The

The Official Guide Book of
The New Lyke Wake Club

A 40 Mile Crossing of
The North York Moors
From Osmotherley to Ravenscar

An Essential Guide to Help you Complete
The Lyke Wake Walk

For Jessica
7/4/07

Walk Guides   **THE YORKSHIRE DALES TOP TEN**
ISBN 978-0-9526900-5-4
THE DERBYSHIRE TOP TEN
ISBN 978-1-903568-03-3
THE COMPLETE ISLE OF WIGHT COASTAL FOOTPATH
ISBN 978-0-9526900-6-1
ISLE OF WIGHT, NORTH TO SOUTH – EAST TO WEST
ISBN 978-1-903568-07-1
THE SCOTTISH COAST TO COAST WALK
ISBN 978-0-9526900-8-5
THE YORKSHIRE 3 PEAKS WALK
ISBN 978-1-903568-46-0
THE YORKSHIRE 3 PEAKS WALK SKETCH MAP & ROUTE GUIDE
ISBN 978-1-903568-23-1
17 WALKS IN GLEN NEVIS
ISBN 978-1-903568-05-7
THE GREAT GLEN WAY
ISBN 978-1-903568-13-2
THE LANCASHIRE TRAIL
ISBN 978-1-903568-10-1
THE 1066 COUNTRY WALK
ISBN 978-1-903568-00-2
THE NATIONAL 3 PEAKS WALK
ISBN 978 1-903568-24-8
SHORT WALKS IN THE LAKE DISTRICT
ISBN 978-1-903568-20-0
JOHN O'GROATS TO LANDS END
ISBN 978-1-903568-18-7
WALK HADRIAN'S WALL
ISBN 978-1-903568-40-8
Tourist Guides   **TOURIST GUIDE TO VARADERO, CUBA**
ISBN 978-1-903568-08-8
EXPLORE – FORT WILLIAM & GLEN NEVIS
ISBN 978-1-903568-25-5
Obtainable from bookshops or direct from the address below.
See web site for book details. **www.chall-pub.co.uk**

THE LYKE WAKE WALK GUIDE
ISBN 978-1-903568-47-7

Third Edition 2007

CHALLENGE PUBLICATIONS
7, EARLSMERE DRIVE, BARNSLEY. S71 5HH

Brian Smailes

Holds the record for the fastest 4 and 5 continuous crossings of the Lyke Wake Walk over the North York Moors. He completed the 210 miles over rough terrain on 5 crossings in June 1995 taking 85 hours and 50 minutes. In 2007 he completed his 51st crossing.

His most recent venture was an expedition to China, walking sections of the Great Wall in remote areas of China and the former borders of Mongolia. On a 2005 expedition, Brian walked the Inca Trail in Peru, visiting Lake Titticacca and Bolivia whilst in the area.

In August 2003 he walked from John O'Groats to Lands End, completing it in 34 days. In August 2001, cycling from Lands End to John O`Groats, a journey of over 910 miles took 6 days 13 hours 18 minutes. This involved carrying food, clothing and tent, and was completed without any support between both ends. A further unsupported cycle ride, this time from John O'Groats to Lands End is planned in 2007 with a target of 5 days.

Having travelled extensively throughout the UK, Europe and the Caribbean, Brian has recently been writing international travel guides to enable the holidaymaker to access the world with ease and enjoy it as much as he does.

Long distance running, canoeing and sub aqua diving are other sports he enjoys, completing 25 marathons and canoeing the Caledonian Canal 3 times. Brian has dived all around the UK coastline as well as Thailand, Cuba and Mexico.

Brian lives in Yorkshire and has walked the hills and dales throughout the County. In compiling this 3rd edition of The Lyke Wake Guide, the route still holds as much pleasure and mystery in walking it again as it did the first time he walked it.

ACKNOWLEDGEMENTS

It is with thanks to the following people for assistance, that this book has been published: -
Pam Smailes
Gerry Orchard
The Lyke Wake Club for information and support.

Brian Smailes is identified as author of this book in accordance with Copyright Act 1988.
No part of this publication may be reproduced by any means without prior permission in writing from the publisher.

First Published 1994
Second Edition 2003
Revised 2004
This Edition 2007
ISBN 978-1-903568-47-7
Published by Challenge Publications, 7, Earlsmere Drive, Ardsley, Barnsley, S71 5HH.
www.chall-pub.co.uk

Printed by Dearne Valley Printers, Wath upon Dearne, Rotherham.

The information recorded in this book is believed by the author to be correct at time of publication. No liabilities can be accepted for any inaccuracies found. Anyone using this guide should refer to their map in conjunction with this book. The description or representation of a route used is not evidence of a right of way.

CONTENTS

PHOTOGRAPHS

THE NEW LYKE WAKE CLUB

The New Lyke Wake Club was reformed on 8th May 2004 taking over from the 'old' Lyke Wake Club, which closed in October 2005, and to preserve the traditions of the founder of the walk, Bill Cowley who died in 1994.

All existing dirgers are entitled to membership of the club and they especially welcome new dirgers, who are people who complete at least one crossing of this famous route as described herein. Those who do complete the walk can purchase a range of souvenirs: -

- **Condolence Cards -** 50p new size
- **Supporters Cards -** for drivers, cooks and bottle washers - 50p
- **Doublecrosser Condolence Cards** - if you do it there
  and back! - 50p
- **Club Badge** - coffin shape, metal pin - £2.50 new size
- **Woven Cloth Badge** - for jackets or rucksacks - £2.30
- **Car Stickers** - £1.25
- **Club Tie** - £9.95
- **Lyke Wake CD** - with 170 photos of the route - £4.00
- **Further copies of this guidebook** - £4.50
- **T-Shirt** - £8.99, black/yellow motif, state size S,M,L,EX
- **Polo shirt** - £12.99, black/yellow motif, state size S,M,L,EX
- **Desk Calendar** - £4.00
- **'Walking The Lyke Wake Walk'** - 58 minute DVD,
  filmed in high definition - £10.00

Prices shown apply in 2007. Check club website for prices and items in future years – www.lykewake.org

All the above are available from Gerry Orchard, 4, Cavendish Grove, Hull Road, York, YO10 3ND Cheques payable to New Lyke Wake Club. When ordering, if you include an e-mail address you will receive the club newsletter at various times throughout the year.

The club is run by a council (committee) whose members live principally in Yorkshire but is open to people from all around the country. The club is a non-profit making body whose stated objectives are: -

- Promoting interest in the North Yorkshire Moors, their history and folklore.
- Assisting in safeguarding the moorland environment.
- Encouraging the sport of long distance walking and running.
- Providing advice and fellowship for those taking part.

The club has social events, which are often in the form of a festive wake. Further details of these, other news, events and more information on the club can be found on the **clubs official website:**

www.lykewake.org

Crossings can be reported to: - Gerry Orchard, Secretary, New Lyke Wake Club, 4, Cavendish Grove, Hull Road, York, YO10 3ND **Crossings can be reported now by e-mail: crossing.report@lykewake.org**

Every person who completes the walk on foot within 24 hours is eligible for membership, which should be reported within 28 days. **There is no membership fee.**

SHORT HISTORY OF THE WALK

The Lyke Wake Walk is a 40-mile crossing of the North York Moors from Osmotherley to Ravenscar. Official starting point is the Lyke Wake Stone, just past the reservoir on the outskirts of Osmotherley at G.R. 470994 and finishing at the Lyke Wake Stone on Beacon Howes (photo12) at Ravenscar G.R. 971012. Originally the walk started in Osmotherley village and finished in Ravenscar, but in order not to disturb residents in both of these villages, the start and finish is now just outside the villages.

Bill Cowley created the walk in 1955, and issued a challenge to walkers to cross the moors on foot from east to west within 24 hours. On 1st October 1955, 10 men and 3 women set out at noon to perform the first crossing. They reached Ravenscar around 10.30 the next day.

The Lyke Wake Club was born; wake - meaning watching over a corpse and lyke – the corpse itself. The emblem of the club is a coffin badge. You may wonder how and why the unusual name and emblem was used. Throughout the moors there are many ancient burial mounds, known as tumulus or howes. While walking you pass by many of them (photos 9 & 10). Because of these burials and because many bodies were carried over the moors, it was appropriate to use the emblem and name for the club.

Since the walk was created, thousands of people have crossed over! Some groups carry empty coffins across, (or are they)? Others get dressed in black. In times when there was considerable snow, people have skied across. Special condolence cards are available for double crossers, i.e. there and back in one walk!

There have been attempts on other multiple crossings, with the record now set at 85 hours 50 minutes for 5 continuous crossings and 74 hours for 4 continuous crossings by myself in 1995.

Our esteemed club secretary Gerry Orchard has completed over 150 crossings and is known as a centenarian.

There are no honorary members of the club; membership is by completing a crossing. Female members are titled Witch and males are titled Dirger. The club is a friendly club and encourages all members to come and join in the wakes and other solemn occasions. Details of these are posted on the clubs official website.

In the 1970's people were crossing at a rate of around 6000 to 10,000 a year. Today we all try to be more environmentally aware and the numbers crossing are at levels, which are sustainable.

The New Lyke Wake Club awards degrees to those who have made multiple crossings of the Lyke Wake Walk and exhibited knowledge of moorland skills and the ethos of the club.

These degrees may be conferred upon candidates considered to meet the following criteria:-

1. **Master or Mistress of Misery.** Complete three crossings, one in reverse direction and demonstrate by inquisition an appreciation of the ethos of the club and a knowledge of moorland skills, (Neckbands: - black)

2. **Doctor of Dolefulness.** Complete four more crossings including a winter crossing between 1st Dec. and 29th Feb. and an unsupported crossing. Also to present a doctoral thesis on a learned subject relevant to the ethos of the club. (Neckbands: - black and purple)

3. Past **Master or Mistress.** Complete fifteen crossings and perform services to the club recognised as exceptional by the council. Be considered capable of finding the way across the moor by day or night, whether drunk or sober without map or compass. (Black and purple boutonniere)

The 2006 annual wake also agreed in principal to establish a further degree of **Purveyor of Purgatory**. This would be awarded to the leaders of parties who had successfully completed at least three crossings with proper regard to safety and to the fragile environment of the North York Moors.

Cleveland Lyke Wake Dirge

This ancient dirge is sung at the club wakes.

This yah neet,this yah neet,
Ivvery neet an' all,
Fire an' fleet an' cannle leet,
An' Christ tak up thy saul.
When thoo frae hence away art passed
Ivvery neet an' all,
Ti whinny moor thoo cums at last,
An' Christ tak up thy saul.

If ivver thoo gav owther hosen or shoon,
Ivvery neet an' all,
Clap thee doon, an' put 'em on,
An' Christ tak up thy saul

Bud if hosen an' shoon thoo nivver gav neean,
Ivvery neet an' all,
T'whinnies'll prick thee sair ti t'beean,
An' Christ tak up thy saul.

Frae whinny moor when thoo art passed
Ivvery neet an' all,
Ti t'brig o' dreead thoo cums at last,
An' Christ tak up thy saul.

If ivver thoo gav o' thy siller an' gowd,
Ivvery neet an' all,
On t'Brig o' Dreead thoo'll finnd footho'd
An' Christ tak up thy saul.

Bud if siller an' gowd thoo nivver gavn eean,
Ivvery neet an' all,
Thoo'll doon, doon tum'le towards hell fleeames,
An' Christ tak up thy saul.

Frae t'brig o' dreead when thoo art passed
Ivvery neet an' all,
Ti t'fleeames o' hell thoo'll cum at last,
An' Christ tak up thy saul

If ivver thoo gav owther bite or sup,
Ivvery neet an' all,
T' fleeames'll nivver catch thee up,
An' Christ tak up thy saul.

Bud if bite or sup thoo nivver gav neean,
Ivvery neet an' all,
T' flames'll bon thee sair ti t'beean,
An' Christ tak up thy saul

Lyke Wake Dirge Dictionary

Fleet = Flame;   Neean = none;   beean = bone;   Bon = burn

The Lyke Wake Dirge is a medieval funeral dirge, which suggests that everyone after death has to make a journey over difficult moor. If you do various good deeds you will pass various obstacles and get to paradise or Ravenscar whichever you happen to be making for at the time.

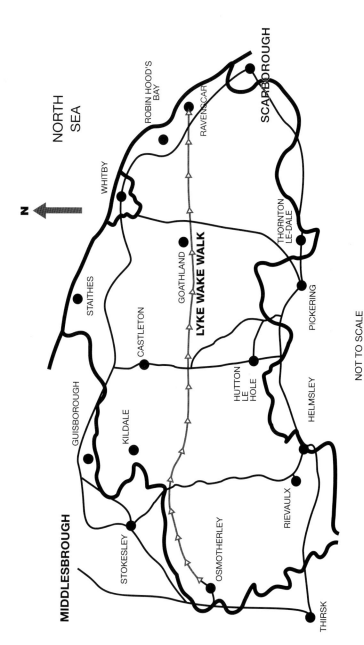

NORTH SEA

MIDDLESBROUGH

SCARBOROUGH

NOT TO SCALE

SKETCH COURTESY OF COLIN WALKER'S SCOUTING MILESTONES
WWW.SCOUTINGMILESTONES@BTINTERNET.CO.UK

N

WHITBY

STAITHES

ROBIN HOOD'S BAY

RAVENSCAR

GOATHLAND

LYKE WAKE WALK

CASTLETON

GUISBOROUGH

KILDALE

THORNTON LE-DALE

PICKERING

HUTTON LE HOLE

HELMSLEY

STOKESLEY

OSMOTHERLEY

RIEVAULX

THIRSK

THE CHALLENGE

The route involves walking 40 miles and includes 5000ft of climbing. The highest point on the walk is Botton Head at 1489ft.

There are good views from the high ground in the first section looking over the flat plains towards Roseberry Topping (photo 5) and towards Middlesbrough.

The route is undulating with a number of short steep climbs up the hillsides and two ravines to descend/ascend (photos 8 & 11), a Roman road to cross and a bog section. When crossing the peat, you either bounce across it, or you can be up to your waist in it, depending on the time of year and recent rainfall.

Just before the halfway point is the disused railway line, 5 miles of cinder track (photo 7), where the wind sweeps up the valley and over the track. There are good views into the valleys of Farndale and Westerdale from the track.

All these challenges make up the Lyke Wake Walk, and this is why people come to experience it and once completed, look forward to wearing the treasured coffin lapel badge with pride!

The crossing is generally considered a hard walk and a challenge to most people. There are seven sections with checkpoints between. Each section presents a different challenge. The first two sections run concurrently with the Cleveland Way before the Lyke Wake turns off east along a disused railway track.

Thousands of people attempt this challenge. Those who prepare beforehand usually succeed those who do not, suffer on route. This book will help everyone, particularly those who may be accepting a challenge for the first time. The walk for many is 40 miles of pure sweat and toil but can be as easy or as hard as you make it.

References to places and roads are taken from the Ordnance Survey maps of North York Moors - Eastern and Western areas No.OL26 and OL27. It is recommended these maps are used with this guide.

LYKE WAKE ELEVATION CHART

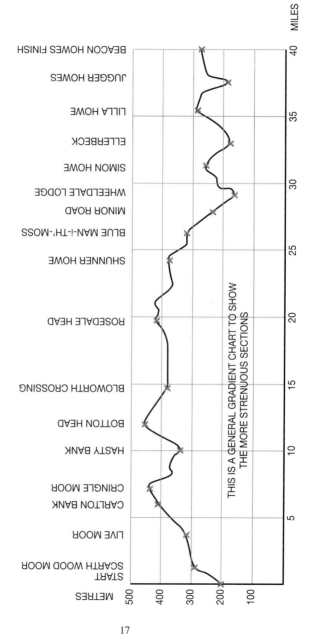

17

Photo 1
Coalmire Plantation on the right. The path turns off right just after the cattle grid into the plantation.

Photo 2
The path leading along Carlton Bank to the 'trig' point just before checkpoint 1. Splendid views from here in daylight.

Photo 3
View from the 'trig' point towards Cringle Moor & Lord Stones Country Park. Our route is either over the hill or around the left side of it.

Photo 4
Looking towards Broughton Plantation & Broughton Bank, with Wain Stones (rocks) top right.

Photo 5
View of the flat plain from Kirby Bank near Broughton Plantation, with Roseberry Topping in the distance.

Photo 6
The track along Broughton Bank leading to Hasty Bank. It can be very muddy after rainfall.

YOUR QUESTIONS ANSWERED

Is the walk tough?

Generally yes, but it is as tough as you make it. If you train and are reasonably fit or used to walking hills and longer distances or jogging, then the walk will seem a lot easier.

Are there any toilets on route?

There are no toilets on route, but there are walls, trees and woods, hills, humps and hollows where you can go when nature calls!

Are there any shops, cafés or other amenities on route?

Virtually none. There is a telephone box at Huthwaite Green.

Beside checkpoint 1 is Lord Stones Café & Country Park. This is an excellent place to stop, depending when you pass. It is generally open between 9am and 5pm but will open at other times by arrangement. They make good bacon sandwiches and a wide selection of other food.

Just before checkpoint 3 is The Lion Inn, ½ mile from Ralphs Cross. They have bar meals etc.

During summer months at weekends, an ice cream van is sometimes based at checkpoint 5 at Fylingdales.

There are no other places on route for food or water, unless you leave the route.

How bad is the boggy section?

Formerly the boggy section was very wet, but over several years it has dried up a lot due to climate changes. It can be wet and you can sink to your knees if you are not careful. Generally it is quite dry in most parts now unless there has been heavy rainfall or snow.

How can I avoid blisters and sore feet?

Follow my recommendations described in 'Boots & Blisters'!

How do I stop my legs from seizing up?

I find the best way is to get some ankle weights and wear them around the house etc. for a few hours each day for a few weeks before you go. Doing this will tone up those muscles. Many people wear light shoes/trainers on their feet then suddenly put on a pair of heavy boots and expect to walk 40 miles. They cannot!

Where can I get badges or other souvenirs of the walk?

Badges and souvenirs are available from Gerry Orchard, secretary, The New Lyke Wake Club, 4 Cavendish Grove, Hull Rd, York YO10 3ND or see the club website at **www.lykewake.org**

PREPARATION

Fitness

Fitness is the most important factor on this walk. People who do some type of training in preparation for this walk succeed; those who drive from A to B and do nothing energetic are more likely to struggle.

Most types of fitness training will help. These include walking jogging, cycling or swimming. A common problem on this walk is upper leg muscle stiffness. Many people wear light shoes on their feet. They then put on a pair of heavy boots and expect to walk 40 miles without the necessary training to tone and build up the upper leg muscles. Result is muscle stiffness and eventually the upper legs seize. Many people have this problem and have to either drop out on route or be closely supported to the nearest checkpoint, so beware!

Food

Food for energy both before and during the walk is essential. Any food containing a high level of carbohydrates consumed the week before the walk and while walking would help in producing energy. High-energy food such as rice, pasta, potato, banana and milk will help to build up energy reserves and enable you to carry on when the going gets tough.

Equipment List

Below is a list of recommended items to take on the walk. The equipment should not prove too expensive and indeed many walkers will already have most of the items on this list. This is only a suggested list and you may wish to vary it to suit your individual requirements.

- Maps - O.S. Explorer OL26 & OL27 North York Moors Eastern & Western areas
- Walking/fell boots
- Stockings/socks - at least 3 pairs
- Gloves
- Woollen hat
- Thin warm jumpers - in layers
- Loose fitting trousers/walking trousers - **not jeans**
- Fleece or Jacket

Photo 7
Walking the old railway line for 5.5 miles to The Lion Inn.

Photo 8
Looking down the steep descent towards Wheeldale Lodge and the stepping stones close by.
Simon Howe is on the horizon.

- Cagoul/anorak/overtrousers (waterproof)
- Complete spare change of clothes
- A pair of soft shoes/trainers for before and after the walk and to be carried in case of problems with boots while walking.
- Basic first aid kit including plasters for blisters and Vaseline for chafing.
- Small 'day' rucksack
- Compass
- Survival bag
- Torch with spare batteries & bulb
- Whistle
- Powder for feet
- Note paper/pencil
- Toilet paper
- Plastic drinks bottles,
- Glucose tablets/sweets
- Camera
- Insect repellent
- Sun/wind cream.

Walking in jeans is inadvisable for three reasons: -
- When jeans get wet they are liable to rub and chafe the skin to the point where you can be extremely sore.
- Wet jeans draw the body heat, which could leave you colder instead of warmer and may result in hypothermia.
- Wet jeans are heavy and take a long time to dry.

Two extremely useful items are a pair of gloves and a woollen hat. Most heat is lost through the back of the head therefore it is prudent to carry a hat or balaclava to help retain your body heat especially in times of cold and wet weather. Because heat is also lost quickly from your extremities, gloves are a useful item to carry.

I recommend travelling to the start in some comfortable trainers or shoes then change into boots at the start of the walk. This means you will only have your boots on for the 12 - 19 hours that it would normally take to complete the crossing.

Throughout this walk there are numerous paths, sheep tracks and farmers paths, which the inexperienced walker could quite easily wander along. Many of the tracks run parallel for a time then gradually lead off in different directions. Basic training in map and compass use would help, especially in the event of bad weather or if attempting the walk on your own or in a small group.

Boots & Blisters

Boots need to be big enough to fit comfortably but not too big so your feet move around inside while walking. Remember to fit the boots with suitable socks when buying.

Sprinkle a liberal quantity of talcum powder on your feet and in the socks. Put talcum powder into your boots and on the outsides of your socks, then put your boots on making sure your feet fit snugly into them. This method has helped many people to keep their feet not only dry and fresh throughout but more importantly blister free after 40 miles.

Change socks at least 3 times on route. Doing this will refresh your feet and provide cushioning. If you feel any warm spots on your feet or toes, do not wait until a blister has formed, change socks, sprinkle foot powder on or put a plaster on.

Remember to cut your toe nails short before you leave home so you don't get any undue pressure on your toes whilst walking or descending hills, which will result in black and painful toenails.

HYPOTHERMIA

Hypothermia is caused when the body core temperature falls below 35°C. If a walker is not properly prepared for the conditions or the clothing worn is not satisfactory, then a combination of the cold, wet, exhaustion and the wind chill factor can give a walker hypothermia.

When you get to a checkpoint then stop walking for a while, you quickly get cold. To combat this, put another layer on, zip up and put gloves and hat on.

The Signs and Symptoms in Descending Order: -
Shivering
Cold, pale and dry skin
Low body temperature
Irrational behaviour
A gradual slip into unconsciousness
Pulse and respiratory rate slow
Difficulty in detecting breathing and pulse when unconscious
Death

Ways of Preventing Hypothermia
1. Build up body clothing in thin layers, adding on or taking off as necessary.
2. Have suitable wind/waterproofs with you.
3. Take some food/hot drink or boiled sweets, which produce energy and heat during digestion.
4. Wear a balaclava/woolly hat to insulate the head, and some gloves.
5. Shelter out of the wind.
6. Take a survival bag and if conditions dictate, use it.

In any type of emergency/accident situation it is always advisable to come off the higher ground as soon as possible especially in low cloud, snow or other bad conditions. The temperature difference between a valley and the high ground can be several degrees.

Treatment for Hypothermia

1. Provide extra clothing and shelter from the elements.
2. Bodily warmth of others helps in a gradual warming.
3. If well enough come down into a warmer sheltered area.
4. Give hot drinks if conscious.
5. Give chocolate or sweets if the patient can still take food.
6. The casualty should be placed so that the head is slightly lower than the body.

DO NOT *rub the skin or use a hot water bottle as this can cause a surge of blood from the central body core to the surface, this could prove fatal.*

Alcohol should not be consumed on any walk and should not be given to anyone who has hypothermia. The body temperature will be lowered as well as giving a false sense of security.

COUNTRYSIDE CODE

1. Be safe – plan ahead and follow any signs
2. Leave gates and property as you find them
3. Protect plants and animals, and take your litter home including any glass
4. Keep dogs under close control
5. Consider other people

The North York Moor is a fragile environment and in hot weather there is the additional risk of devastating fire. Do not light fires in or near the moorland and ensure that all cigarettes are extinguished.

In times of drought, the moors are sometimes closed due to the fire risk. The New Lyke Wake Club suggests that walk organisers check the current position via the club website at www.lykewake.org or that of the North York Moors National Park Authority.

The New Lyke Wake Club and The North York Moors National Park suggest that groups be small and not exceeding 10 people.

ON ROUTE ENCOUNTERS

Throughout the walk there are numerous items of interest. I will describe these in order of passing.

When starting on the outskirts of Osmotherley you will see the Lyke Wake Stone on a small mound just past the cattle grid on the left opposite the car park.

Through Coalmire Plantation soon after starting (photo 1), you may see deer, fox and numerous rabbits. These animals have been sighted on many occasions.

On Carlton Bank 5.5 miles into your journey there are excellent views from the top (photo 2) and along to the triangulation pillar (front cover). These include Bilsdale television mast, which is a landmark to the southeast. Middlesborough and the Cleveland area can also be seen clearly from the top. On the right as you walk up to the 'trig' point, you pass the Gliding Club.

Even more awe inspiring are the views from the top of Drake Howe on Cringle Moor (photo 3). At a height of 432m the panoramic view is spectacular. On a clear day Penshaw Monument near Sunderland can be seen over 60 miles away to the north.

Proceeding towards checkpoint 2 you will pass a wooden seat near the far end of Broughton Plantation as you descend Hasty Bank. This has an inscription on it, which you should read then proceed with vigour to the checkpoint!

Near Ralph Crosses at Rosedale Head, on your left by the roadside is an unusual boundary stone named White Cross, commonly known as Fat Betty. It is one of the line of boundary stones but individually distinctive.

Water, Water, everywhere! Depending on the conditions and time of year you may find yourself up to the knees in black slimy peat or bouncing over it as you walk. Thankfully though over the last decade the boggy section between Ralph Crosses and Shunner Howe has dried considerably to what it was many years ago. After passing several tumuli on your right, you arrive at Shunner Howe, near checkpoint 4. This area has many tumuli on the moors.

A pleasant sight as you proceed is the scenery and the general area around the old roman road. This leads quickly down to Wheeldale Beck (photo 8). Many people stop here for picnics or to bathe their feet in the beck near the stepping-stones. The village of Goathland, known to many as Aidensfield in Heartbeat, is 3 miles from here.

When you make the long slow climb up towards the high ground and Simon Howe, 260m (photo 9), you will see the new Fylingdales military area from the top. The old 'golf balls' were removed in May 1994. Checkpoint 5 at Eller Beck is another popular place for picnics near the bridge but beware of the busy road.

Before checkpoint 6 is Lilla Howe (photo 10). This is a raised earth mound on the hill supporting a cross, and an early example of Christian Sculpture dated back to Edwin, King of Northumbria in 633 AD.

On reaching this point there are good views of Beacon Howes, Scarborough and the sea. Grouse are often seen not only in this area but also throughout the length of the walk.

Jugger Howe ravine, (photo 11) is an intrepid sight from the top. Located 1mile before checkpoint 6, to traverse both sides of this steep and potentially dangerous ravine and have the energy left to complete the last 3 miles is a daunting task for any walker.

Eventually you arrive at the Lyke Wake Stone at Beacon Howes near Ravenscar (photo 12). If you have enough energy, walk to your left of the radio beacon and look over the cliff. Good views of Robin Hoods Bay and the surrounding area can be seen from here.

Within 3 miles of the finish there are some local public houses including the Falcon Inn, Flask Inn and the Raven Hall Hotel. The famous Smugglers Inn is only 0.5 miles south of Beacon Howes.

Photo 9

Simon Howe with its small standing stones encircling it and Fylingdales military base behind.

Photo 10

Lilla Cross on the Lilla Howe. Reputedly the oldest Christian sculpture in Northern England.

Photo 11

Jugger Howes and steep descent to the beck and footbridge followed by a steep ascent.

Photo 12

The end in sight as you walk over Stony Marl Moor towards the mast near Ravenscar at Beacon Howes.

THE WALKING ROUTE

Start at the Lyke Wake Stone on the outskirts of Osmotherley just past the end of the reservoir opposite sheepwash car park. Time for this 1st section of 6 miles is approx. 2 hrs based on a total walking time of 13 hrs 45 mins, not including stops at checkpoints.

Proceed up the hillside from the Lyke Wake Stone at G.R.470993 then turn right and easterly along Scarth Wood Moor at the top continuing for a short distance until the path descends to meet the metalled road. Cross the road by the cattle grid (photo 1), and through the gate at the far side into Coalmire Plantation. Continue on the path then track for 460m before descending a steep path near the two seats on your left. At the bottom take your second turning right at the signpost. Proceed for 550m until you arrive at a gate on your left with a field beyond. Cross the field then stream at the far side below, then proceed up the metalled road at Hollin Hill to the telephone box at Huthwaite Green. Go through the gate near the telephone box and continue on the path, which gradually winds along at the lower side of Live Moor Plantation and through a gate.

Further on, the path leads to a gate then a set of stone steps, which rise steeply. These are at various heights and lengths. Because of the awkward and uneven step and the total number, together with the height climbed, most walkers feel temporarily exhausted on reaching the top. Although the steps help to combat erosion, they can be dangerous especially when wet or covered in moss.

Completing the steps challenge, you leave the tree line with the wind probably getting stronger as you go through a gate to start the steady climb up Live Moor to 315m, on a stone slabbed path. This eventually leads up (photo 2), to the triangulation pillar on Carlton Bank (front cover) at a height of 408m. Care needs to be taken especially on this first section while the body adapts to the conditions and changing temperature. More importantly can be the difference in weather, from no wind at the start to gale force winds at the summit on Carlton Bank with low cloud and extreme cold. The glider base near the top on the right is a useful landmark but keep to the path along the left side (photo 2) up to the triangulation pillar. Walk ahead and head down a path (photo 3) which

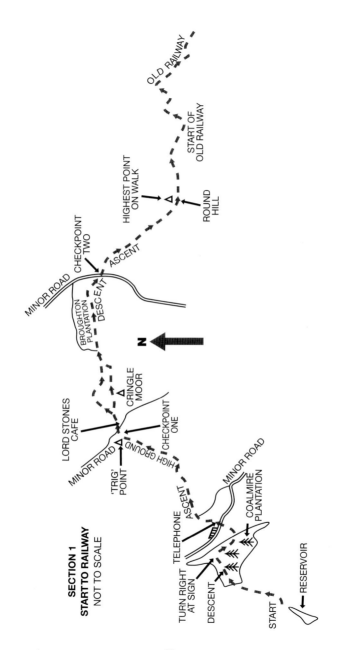

SECTION 1
START TO RAILWAY
NOT TO SCALE

OLD RAILWAY

START OF
OLD RAILWAY

ROUND
HILL

HIGHEST POINT
ON WALK

ASCENT

CHECKPOINT
TWO

MINOR ROAD

DESCENT

BROUGHTON
PLANTATION

N

CRINGLE
MOOR

LORD STONES
CAFE

'TRIG'
POINT

MINOR ROAD

HIGH GROUND

CHECKPOINT
ONE

TELEPHONE

ASCENT

MINOR ROAD

TURN RIGHT
AT SIGN

COALMIRE
PLANTATION

DESCENT

START

RESERVOIR

is steep and rocky in places to arrive at checkpoint one, entrance to Carlton Bank Glider Club at the road.

Near the minor road crossing at checkpoint one is Lord Stones Café just around the bend. Excellent food and drinks are available during the daytime.

Section two of the walk takes approximately 1 hr 30 mins and is 4 miles long. After leaving checkpoint one there are two directions you can take. Cross the stile from the road then walk through Lord Stones Country Park towards Drake Howe.

The first route takes you up a direct path, which is very steep but leads straight to the top of Drake Howe (hilltop) on Cringle Moor (photo 3) at 432m. Once on top there are excellent views, up to 60 miles on a clear day. Continue along the path on the top and down at the far side before proceeding along the track at the right side of the forest known as Broughton Plantation (photo 3).

The alternative route that can be used particularly in bad weather is a path around the left side of Cringle Moor. This path is undulating and may have some water and springs appearing as you proceed around it. There are also good views from here (photo 5). Access is on a worn path, bearing left at the stone wall at the bottom of the hill. Whichever route you choose you will arrive at Broughton Plantation with a path ascending the right side of it.

On arriving at Broughton Plantation go down a short steep ditch or dike beside two stone posts and back up the other side, then go through a gate, where the plantation begins. Most walkers walk on the ascending track by the side of the plantation, though some prefer to traverse along the high, exposed peaks on your right (photo 4).

The track alongside the plantation can be very wet and muddy (photo 6), with many stones interspersed along the route. Because there is a stone wall on one side and forest on the other, this stretch is generally quite sheltered. This section is usually considered a good toilet stop! Toilet stops are generally few and far between. Stay on this undulating track for 2 miles.

Just before arriving at checkpoint two you descend a long steep hill called Hasty Bank where the track widens. Here you will see a seat on your right side. Bear right just past the seat, after reading the inscription on it, and go down the stone steps at the side of the wall to checkpoint two on Clay Bank Road.

Section three is the longest section and takes approximately 3 hrs for this 9.5 mile route. Cross the road then go through a gate followed by a steep climb up Carr Ridge on Urra Moor. On the top, as you go through another gate, the path is seen to be winding into the distance. This path leads to Round Hill at Botton Head, which is the highest point on the whole walk, 454m. Following this old path for a further 2km leads you to the old railway line. When you see the railway line bear right at the marker post, on a narrow path leading up to the old railway line 800m further. This point is called Bloworth Crossing, at 410m

This railway track is the main challenge in this section. When walking on the old railway line (photo 7), it can be very windy as the wind sweeps up the valley and over the embankments. Ensure you carry suitable wind/ waterproof clothing whilst walking on this exposed track.

Continue in an easterly direction on the flat track for 5 miles and you come to Blakey Moor. Look for the orange/red roof of the Lion Inn on the higher ground on Blakey Ridge, where there is a short path off on your left up Cockpit Hill to The Lion Inn at 400m. Turn left on the road by The Lion Inn and head for Ralph Crosses T-junction at Rosedale Head where checkpoint three is a small parking area.

Prepare at checkpoint three for wet feet because the challenge in this next section is the peat bogs. This 5 mile section usually takes around 2 hrs to complete but wet or dry conditions can affect your travelling time by quite a lot.

Turn right from Ralph Crosses and walk along the road towards Rosedale Abbey for nearly 2 miles. Just after leaving Rosedale Head, on your left is a curious white painted stone called Fat Betty. The road is reasonably flat so gives the legs some relief. You pass a minor road on your left, then after approximately 200m, turn left onto an ascending stony path that is not well marked.

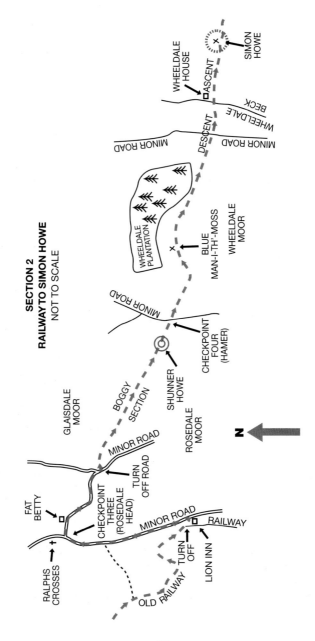

SECTION 2
RAILWAY TO SIMON HOWE
NOT TO SCALE

SIMON HOWE

WHEELDALE HOUSE

ASCENT

WHEELDALE BECK

MINOR ROAD

DESCENT

MINOR ROAD

WHEELDALE PLANTATION

BLUE MAN-I-TH'-MOSS

WHEELDALE MOOR

MINOR ROAD

CHECKPOINT FOUR (HAMER)

SHUNNER HOWE

BOGGY SECTION

GLAISDALE MOOR

ROSEDALE MOOR

N

MINOR ROAD

TURN OFF ROAD

FAT BETTY

CHECKPOINT THREE (ROSEDALE HEAD)

MINOR ROAD

RAILWAY

TURN OFF

RALPHS CROSSES

LION INN

OLD RAILWAY

36

Experience has shown that to travel fairly light over this short section, if weather conditions permit, would help. The reason for this is because there are a number of dikes or ditches that you must cross. These are often full of water or unstable peat. To enable you to cross the boggy area easier, leave heavy rucksacks and equipment with the back up team but retain waterproof and spare warm clothing with you. I must emphasis that this should only be done in times of good weather and with a reliable support team to meet you at checkpoint four.

Cross from the roadside on to a worn path on your left. This can be difficult to find as you leave the road. Once over the brow of the hill and past the 'trig' point there at 432m, you will be walking on thick peat. When dry you tend to bounce across, when wet you sink into it. There are natural springs, which come to the surface so the ground is very wet in parts with reed beds and surface water or black wet peat where you can sink in sometimes when you least expect it.

The path from leaving the road to checkpoint four just past Shunner Howe is a direct straight line, with white painted marker stones along the route, so not hard to follow except in fog or snow. Continue until you meet a road, where the checkpoint is nearby. This is known as Hamer.

The next section to checkpoint five is approximately 8.5 miles and takes around 3 hrs for this demanding stretch from Hamer to Eller Beck on the Pickering to Whitby road. Many people say this section is more than 9 miles long. This is usually because they are often feeling stiff by this time and walking at a slower pace.

The challenge in this section is the steep ravine, which the unsuspecting walkers suddenly find themselves at the top of (photo 8). Before you arrive at the ravine you have, in parts, a difficult path to follow. When you leave Hamer at checkpoint four, the path is quite well defined and can be wet and peaty for the 1st mile. Head for the high ground ahead called 'Blue Man i 'th' Moss' in a generally easterly direction. Once on the higher ground near a large standing stone, the path then becomes very rock strewn and difficult to navigate over, as well as being hard to follow. The narrow path swings right after passing the higher ground.

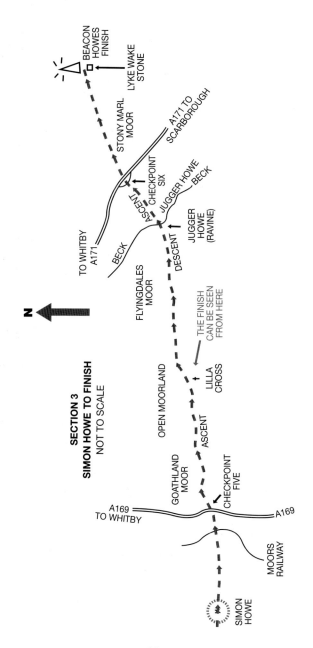

SECTION 3
SIMON HOWE TO FINISH
NOT TO SCALE

N

BEACON
HOWES
FINISH

LYKE WAKE
STONE

STONY MARL
MOOR

A171 TO
SCARBOROUGH

CHECKPOINT
SIX

ASCENT

JUGGER HOWE
BECK

TO WHITBY
A171

BECK

DESCENT

JUGGER
HOWE
(RAVINE)

FLYINGDALES
MOOR

THE FINISH
CAN BE SEEN
FROM HERE

LILLA
CROSS

OPEN MOORLAND

ASCENT

GOATHLAND
MOOR

A169
TO WHITBY

CHECKPOINT
FIVE

A169

MOORS
RAILWAY

SIMON
HOWE

Wheeldale Plantation is approximately 500m to your left. You will see it as you proceed along the rocky path but keep the forest line off to your left at a distance. At the time of writing, forestry work is being done to fell the trees in some parts. The narrow stony path continues until you cross Wheeldale Road and the terrain changes to more picturesque scenery.

Cross a stile and proceed down the right side of a field that has been reclaimed from moorland. Here you cross the remains of a Roman road and see the steep ravine you have to descend to get to the beck near Wheeldale Lodge (photo 8).

While descending the hillside look across to see your path on the far side. Cross the stepping-stones over Wheeldale Beck at the bottom and ascend the other side on a steady climb to Simon Howe at 260m and the circle of stones there (photo 9). At this point you may see checkpoint five ahead at Fylingdales and good views of all the surrounding area.

A long descent brings you to the railway line of the North York Moors Railway. You may even see the steam train on its regular journey from Grosmont to Pickering. Cross over the line and up the bank to checkpoint five at Eller Beck Bridge. There is only 7 miles to complete now. It is advisable to consume food and drink quickly here then continue before the legs become too stiff!

Section five takes you across the busy A169 road. Follow a path from the far side of the stone bridge at the bend in the road for approx. 2.3 miles. This leads along the side of Little Eller Beck (stream) and skirts around the military area of Fylingdales. Bear right onto a man made stony access road on Lilla Rigg, heading for the mound on the highest ground ahead (Lilla Howe), along the northwest side of the military area. Go through a 5-bar gate, on the military access road before a short ascent over sometimes boggy ground to arrive beside Lilla Cross on the top of Lilla Howe (photo 10). At this point you have excellent views of the surrounding area, also of the mast, which is the finish point, (photo 12).

The path gradually descends at the far side over Burn Howe on High Moor, and after 2 miles you again find yourself at the top of a ravine (photo 11). This is Jugger Howe ravine, and at the bottom a narrow platform bridge crosses the beck. There is a steep ascent on the far side before it leads onto a gravel path then an old army road to checkpoint six, which is Jugger Howes at 210m, near the Flask Inn on the Whitby/Scarborough road.

You will probably find at this stage that it is better to continue on to the finish rather than stop here for refreshments and possibly seize up.

This section will take approximately 30 mins as you cross the busy main A171 road with extreme care and up a short, steep embankment on to Stony Marl Moor, then it is a straight path in a north easterly direction for 2 miles to finish at the Lyke Wake Stone at Beacon Howes by the mast (photo 12) at 266m.

Celebrations are in order if you have enough energy, otherwise take a well-earned rest!

SUPPORT TEAM

Most people usually attempt this walk from Osmotherley to Ravenscar with a support team who will meet them at each checkpoint and provide food and drinks. It is important to remember that if you are a walker you should keep in mind the distance between each checkpoint and the approximate time to complete the section. Consider your physical and mental state as you progress to each checkpoint and the weather conditions. You should then be able to decide whether you can continue to the next checkpoint or retire honourably at the one you are at.

A good support team who give verbal encouragement as well as hot food and drinks are essential for all walkers. When arriving at a checkpoint, walkers should not have to wait for food and drinks. These should be ready as the walkers arrive. Too long spent at a checkpoint will result in walkers feeling stiff, cold and tired. As the walk progresses the time spent at a checkpoint becomes more critical as the body becomes stiffer.

Walkers should arrive at a checkpoint, be fed and watered and set off again within 15 mins if possible. On this walk, most walkers get to at least the halfway stage and often to checkpoint 4 at Hamer, before some start to drop out. This is usually due to stiff legs, fatigue and blisters, but there may be other problems like sprained ankles, badly fitting boots or hypothermia. A good support team will anticipate these problems and be ready to deal with them.

A good safety precaution is for the backup team to operate a checking in system at each checkpoint. Walkers should report to their car or mini-bus driver at each checkpoint and be marked off on a walkers register. Taking this precaution should ensure no walker has gone astray between checkpoints.

All support teams must have an adequate supply of first aid equipment particularly adhesive plasters. They should also carry sleeping bags for any possible hypothermia cases and torches with spare batteries for any emergency at night.

Support teams should have one person who is familiar with the walk and understands the problems the walkers face in each section. There may be a need to go along the route to retrieve or assist a tired or injured walker. An emergency rucksack with the necessary equipment in should be ready. This pack should include some food and drink, note pad, pen, first aid pack, a windproof, warm clothing and survival bag.

Many people have mobile telephones, but often they do not function in hilly areas and in a 7-mile radius of Fylingdales. It is good to take mobiles, but they are not guaranteed to work, so do not rely on them.

Another option would be to take CB radios or similar. Again, they may not work in hilly areas, but will work in many areas.

The success or failure of individuals or the whole group depends in some situations on how good the support team are overall and if they are at exactly the right place at the right time. This is sometimes a problem in thick fog! A good support team should have a responsible project leader who will have basic first aid skills and be a competent map reader.

SUPPORT TEAM DRIVING ROUTE

Start at the first car park on the right just past the cattle grid after leaving Osmotherley, near the Lyke Wake Stone.

From the car park, North for 2 miles to A172, and turn right. After a further 2 miles turn right again and head through Carlton in Cleveland and up the hill, a total of 6 miles to: -

CHECKPOINT 1 - CARLTON BANK
Side of the road at top of hill with small signpost 'CAFE' on left. Glider club entrance is on right side by a barrier.

Continue on same road to B1257, at Chop Gate 4.2 miles, turn left and head north a further 2.4 miles to: -

CHECKPOINT 2 - HASTY BANK
Lay-by on both sides before the corner (trees on left). Steps down left side of forest. Gate on right side of road.

Continue north from lay-by and first turning right to Ingleby Greenhow 2 miles, and Battersby 1.5 miles and Kildale a further 2 miles all in a northeasterly direction. 1.5 miles after Kildale, head southeast to Westerdale 3.5 miles and a further 2.5 miles to: -

CHECKPOINT 3 - RALPH CROSSES (Rosedale Head)
Gravel car park on corner at the junction.

Head southeast to Rosedale Abbey a distance of 5.5 miles, turn left at public house in village and head northeast for 3 miles to: -

CHECKPOINT 4 - HAMER
A wide path on left and one on the right. Grass and parking area at the side of the road.

Continue north east for 6 miles to Egton Bridge and east for 1.5 miles to Grosmont, head east and then south-east for 2 miles to A169, turn right and south for 4 miles to: -

CHECKPOINT 5 - ELLER BECK
Lay-by on right just above bridge.

Head back north on the same road towards Sleights and after 4.5 miles turn right and east to Littlebeck, 1 mile. Continue east to join B1416 after 1 mile. Continue on this road and join A171. Turn right and head south for 3 miles to: -

CHECKPOINT 6 - JUGGER HOWES
1.5 miles past Flask Inn turn right into lay-by on right at top of hill. Padlocked gate and stile there.

On leaving, turn right on same road for 2 miles then turn left to Ravenscar. After 1 mile turn left at junction and head northwest to finish at: -

CHECKPOINT 7 - BEACON HOWES (G.R. 971012)
Radio mast on high ground near Ravenscar and the Lyke Wake Stone (photo 12) finish

USEFUL INFORMATION

Recommended Maps
OS North York Moors Explorer no. OL26 (western area)
OS North York Moors Explorer no. OL27 (eastern area)

Mileage & Walking Times from Osmotherley to Ravenscar

Checkpoint	Miles	Walk Time
Start – 1	6	2 hours
1 – 2	4	1 hour 30 mins
2 – 3	9.5	3 hours 5 mins
3 – 4	5	2 hours
4 – 5	8.5	3 hours
5 – 6	5	1 hour 40 mins
6 – Finish	2	30 mins
Total	40	

Based on an approximate walking time of 13 hrs 45 mins, not including breaks at checkpoints. Actual walking times vary depending on the number of walkers and the conditions at the time of walking.

When attempting this challenging walk it is advisable to start around midnight while you are feeling fresh and finish around 4-6pm when you are exhausted but with daylight left. This is even more important during winter months when it gets dark earlier. Leave enough time to finish in daylight allowing extra time at the end for varying weather and walking conditions.

Alternatively, you could start at first light if walking during May to July. Doing this would mean you do not miss the best scenery from the start to just past checkpoint 2 as it will be daylight.

When driving through Osmotherley during unsocial hours, do not stop or make noise in the village but drive directly to the start outside the village.

Weather conditions throughout the walk can vary considerably. A calm, still evening in Osmotherley can turn into gale force winds on the tops and torrential rain on route.

Distances to Nearest Villages

			Miles	Kms
Start Point	to	Osmotherley	1	1.6
Checkpoint 1	to	Carlton in Cleveland	1.25	2
Checkpoint 2	to	Great Broughton	2.9	4.7
Checkpoint 3	to	Castleton	4	6.4
Checkpoint 4	to	Egton Bridge	5	8
Checkpoint 5	to	Pickering	10.5	16.9
Checkpoint 6	to	Whitby	10	16.1
Beacon Howes	to	Ravenscar	1	1.6

Grid References on Route

These grid references can be used to programme your GPS before you walk or to identify the route on a map.

Start at LW Stone	**G.R.**470993
Coalmire Plantation	473004
Viewpoint in Plantation near the Descen	479006
Huthwaite Green by Telephone Box	493007
Path on Live Moor	503013
Path on Carlton Bank	517022
'Trig' Point on Carlton Bank	519026
Checkpoint 1	523030
Broughton Plantation	547035
Checkpoint 2	573033
Track near Botton Head	594015
Bloworth Crossing	616015
Turn off Railway to The Lion Inn	675997
Checkpoint 3 Rosedale Head	677019
Turning off Road to Bog Section	698011
Shunner Howe	737997
Checkpoint 4 Hamer	744995
Path near Wheeldale Plantation	777991
Minor Road near the Roman Road	804983
Wheeldale Beck	812982

Simon Howe	830981
Checkpoint 5 Eller Beck	857982
Path by Little Eller Beck	874986
Lilla Cross on Lilla Howe	889987
Path to Jugger Howe	915992
Jugger Howe Ravine	931994
Checkpoint 6	945002
Path Leading to the Mast	955007
Beacon Howes/LW Stone	970012

Heights Climbed

	Feet	Metres
Lyke Wake Stone	676	206
Scarth Wood Moor	981	299
Live Moor	1033	315
Carlton Bank	1338	408
Cringle Moor	1417	432
Hasty Bank	1115	340
Botton Head	1489	454
Bloworth Crossing	1286	392
Rosedale Head	1371	418
Loose Howe	1417	432
Shunner Howe	1214	370
Blue Man i 'th'Moss	1046	319
Minor Road	751	229
Wheeldale Lodge	554	169
Simon Howe	853	260
Eller Beck Bridge	584	178
Lilla Howe	951	290
Jugger Howes	623	190
Beacon Howes	873	266

Accommodation on Route

Accommodation is limited throughout the route generally. The following places are not listed in any order of priority other than route order.

B&B

Vane House,   (G.R. SE 457973)
11a North End
Osmotherley DL6 3BA
01609 883448
www.vanehouse.co.uk   allan@vanehouse.co.uk

Hotel
Golden Lion Hotel
6, West End,
Osmotherley, DL6 3AA
01609 883526
Bar, Food, Accommodation
www.goldenlionosmotherley.co.uk

Camping & Youth Hostel
Cote Ghyll   (G.R. SE 461981)
Osmotherley.
0870 770 5982

Camping by arrangement.
Lord Stones Café & Country Park,
Carlton Bank,
Chop Gate,
Nr. Stokesley,
01642 778227

Camping Facilities & B&B
The Lion Inn   (G.R. SE 679997)
Blakey Ridge
Kirkbymoorside, YO62 7LQ
01751 417320
www.lionblakey.co.uk   lionblakey@virgin.net

Camping Barn
Farndale Camping Barn,   Sleeps 12 (G.R. SE 659986)
Mr & Mrs Mead,
Oak House,
Farndale,
Kirkbymoorside, YO62 7LH
01751 433053

B&B
Falcon Inn,   (G.R. SE 972981)
Whitby Road,
Near Cloughton,
Scarborough, YO13 0DY
01723 870717
Bar, Food & Accommodation
www.yorkshirecoast.co.uk/falcon

Hotel
Raven Hall Hotel,   (G.R. NZ. 981018)
Ravenscar,
Scarborough, YO13 0ET
01723 870353
Bar, Food & Accommodation
www.ravenhall.co.uk

Group Hire
Ravenscar Village Hall,
Mrs. V. Russell,
Ravenhurst,
Church Road,
Ravenscar, YO13 0LZ
01723 870801

National Park & Tourist Information Centres

Sutton Bank Visitor Centre,
Sutton Bank,
Thirsk,
YO7 2EH
01845 597426

The Moors National Park Centre,

Danby,
Whitby,
YO21 2NB
01439 772737

Malton T.I.C.
at Malton Museum,

Market Place,
Malton,
YO17 7LP
01653 600048

Thirsk T.I.C.

49, Market Place,
Thirsk,
YO7 1HA
01845 522755

Whitby T.I.C.

Langbourne Road,
Whitby,
YO21 1YN
01947 604679

Helmsley T.I.C.

at Helmsley Castle Visitor Centre,
Castle Gate,
Helmsley,
YO62 5AB
01439 770173

Pickering T.I.C.
at The Ropery,
Pickering,
YO18 8DY
01751 473791

Scarborough T.I.C.
Brunswick Shopping Centre,
Westborough,
Scarborough,
YO11 1UE
01723 383636/7

Public Houses & Cafés on Route
Osmotherley – Golden Lion Hotel
Osmotherley – Queen Catherine
Lord Stones Café and Country Park
Blakey Ridge – The Lion Inn
Nearby the Finish – The Falcon Inn
Osmotherley walking shop is situated in the village centre if you forget any equipment or need new items.

Useful Addresses
Teesdale & Weardale Mountain Rescue team linked to Cleveland Search & Rescue team request that groups leave details of their walk on the website which is www.mytrips.org.uk This will help them to find and rescue any group or individual who may be lost or injured on the moors.

Long Distance Walkers Association
Paul Lawrence,
15, Tamarisk Rise,
Wokingham,
Berkshire RG40 1WG
Tel: 01189 790190

This association is set up to further the interests of those who enjoy long distance walking. Members receive a journal three times each year, (strider), which includes information on all aspects of long distance walking.
Website – www.ldwa.org.uk.   **e-mail** LDP@ldwa.org.uk

Ramblers Association
2nd Floor, Camelford House,
87-90 Albert Embankment,
London SE1 7TW
Tel: 01577 861222
Advice and information on all walking matters. Local groups with regular meetings.

Lord Stones Café & Country Park,
Carlton Bank,
Chop Gate,
Nr. Stokesley,
Middlesbrough
TS9 7JH
Tel 01642 778227

The Countryside Agency for England
www.countryside.gov.uk/access

North York Moors National Park Website
www.moors.uk.net

Glossary of Words

Bearing - A degree or number of degrees set on a compass; follow the direction of travel arrow walking on that bearing to reach your intended destination.

Beck – A stream or brook.

Crag - A steep rugged rock or peak.

Dirger – A mourner who attends a wake and follows the corpse from home to church.

Grid Reference - Derived from the national grid reference system. This is used to pinpoint a place on a map by use of letters and numbers.

Howe - A burial mound usually encircled by stones.

Kissing Gate - Swing gate that usually lets one person through it at a time by moving the gate backwards and forwards.

Lyke – The corpse itself. Derived from a German word lych, also meaning the gateway to the church, where a coffin would be laid initially.

Lyke Way – Is the path by which a corpse was moved from its resting place to church.

Magnetic Bearing - This is a grid bearing taken from a map and the relevant magnetic variation added to it to obtain the magnetic bearing. See the relevant maps for details of current magnetic variation.

Path – A walkway or route usually under two metres wide.

Resurrectionist – Is an 18c bodysnatcher who removed bodies for medical schools.

Summit - The highest point of a mountain or hill.

Track – A route more than two metres wide.

Trig Point - True name is Triangulation Pillar. These mark the summit of many mountains, but not all. It is a small stone pillar with a number on it. The height of the mountain is taken from this point. There are trig points on Botton head, the highest point on the walk, and at Carlton Bank

Tumulus – Ancient sepulchral or burial mound.

Wake – Watching over a corpse overnight.

The route described in this book was used by the author in 2007 and believed to be correct at the time of publication. Hopefully you have enjoyed your crossing and gained as much pleasure from walking the route as he did. Remember, the first time is always the worst: it gets easier after that! Should you wish to walk other challenging routes, please visit Challenge Publications website at: -

www.chall-pub.co.uk

Or the new National 3 Peaks website

www.national3peaks.co.uk

A wide selection of walking guides covering the UK are available including The National 3 Peaks Walk, Hadrian's Wall, The Yorkshire 3 Peaks Walk and John O'Groats to Lands End. These books, like the others produced, contain everything you need to know to complete the challenge. See list in front of book.

On our website you will find other interesting, and possibly different walks around the British Isles, which are equally as picturesque and enjoyable as this one.

Should you wish to comment on this book or give further information to help keep the book updated then please write to the address below or e-mail via the website. An acknowledgement will be given: -

Please write to: -

Challenge Publications

7, Earlsmere Drive,

Ardsley,

Barnsley.

S71 5HH

THE END

Notes